MESSAGES

Other works from Serpent Club Press:

2013
Moon on Water
Matthew Gasda

2014
Autumn, Again; Spring, Anew
Michael Skelton and Stephen Morel

On Bicycling: An Introduction
Samuel Atticus Steffen

2015
Sonata for Piano and Violin
Matthew Gasda

New Writing: Volume 1
A Compilation

Forthcoming in 2015…
Circumambulate
Daniel Bossert

MESSAGES

A play by Matthew Gasda

Serpent Club Press

First Edition

Printed in the United States of America
Set in Williams Caslon
Designed by Emily Gasda

ISBN
9780990664352

LCCN
2015911563

MESSAGES

Characters:

MAISIE, *a musician*
EMILY, *a painter and MAISIE's roommate*
MAX, *a youthful writer*
DAVID, *a handsome, self-assured New Yorker in his 30's*

Messages was first presented by Gorilla Repertory Theater Company in January 2015 at the studio of Benjamin Heller in Brooklyn, NY, with the following cast:

MAISIE	Timothy Laurel Harrison
EMILY	Chelsea LeSage
MAX	Charles Munn
DAVID	Leajato Robinson

Directed by Christopher Carter Sanderson, with Greg Petroff as Stage Manager.

Messages was again presented by Gorilla Repertory Theater Company in July 2015, as part of the Midtown International Theater Festival at the Davenport Theater at 354 West 45th Street, New York, NY, with the following cast:

MAISIE	Hannah Wolff
EMILY	Chelsea LeSage
MAX	Jonathan Reed Wexler
DAVID	Leajato Robinson

Directed by Christopher Carter Sanderson, with Greg Petroff as Stage Manager.

Setting

Common area of bohemian loft apartment: floor length window, high ceiling, large farm-style kitchen table, piles of books and records, film posters on the walls, various unfinished art projects propped against the walls, a large futon, and kitchenette with cupboards and gas range, with a tea kettle on one of the burners.

Doors that 'lead' to characters' bedrooms can be placed as needed.

The entire action of the play takes place within Maisie and Emily's apartment.

The play is divided into numbered acts, which indicate a change of time. The time is the present.

ACT I

The STAGE is dark.

Cue: Rain FX

The lights come up slightly, mimicking early morning light.

Rain FX fade.

OFFSTAGE someone begins to play a few bars from Stravinsky's 'Elegy' for solo viola. The playing is fragmented and wistful: the sound of a gifted musician who has not practiced for a long time.

The lights continue to brighten.

The viola playing stops.

Enter MAISIE.

MAISIE goes to the kitchenette where she fills the teakettle and places it on the burner.

While the kettle is boiling, MAISIE gets a book and sits down at the table.

Enter MAX.

MAX sits across from MAISIE and the two continue in silence for a few moments.

MAISIE puts the book down and looks at MAX.

Silence.

MAX reaches for the book, looks at the table and pushes it back to the middle of the table.

Silence.

MAX

What did you think of the poem?

MAISIE

I'm not sure why you wanted me to read it.

MAX

It's pretty obvious, I think—

MAISIE

I don't think it's obvious.

MAX

You just don't want it to be obvious.

MAISIE

That's true.

MAX

A poem makes emotions audible.

MAISIE

Emotions make me nervous.

MAX

    (pushing the book to her)
Read something to me.

MAISIE

No!

MAX

Come on.

MAISIE

It's too early to be romantic!

MAX

I just wanna hear what your voice sounds like—

MAISIE

You know what my voice sounds like.

MAX

You know what I mean—

MAISIE

I don't know what anything means right now.

MAX

Maisie—

MAISIE

If I read something, will you shut up?

MAX

Yes.

MAISIE picks up the book and looks for a page.

MAISIE

Enclosed in seams of white, the song's ellipse/ Of choral blues and diaphonic waves/ Evades the ocean's will, the rhythmic tides/ And brings us to the sea's periphery/ And you comb moons of coral in your hair/ With muted flowers plucked beneath the floors/ Of sealed stars, suspended in your tides/ And lifted in the tally of your love/ For the scarred ports of death open to you/ And wind you into light across the sea/ Of vast white circuits silent in the sound / Of your interwoven many-folded shell/ And in the crossings of our syllables/ I close with you in fragments of the surf/ The flow of all your sea-born voices fuse/ Into the imaged echo of your eyes.

 MAISIE puts the book down.

MAISIE (cont'd)
 Are you happy?

MAX
 More or less.

MAISIE
 This feels unrealistic.

MAX
 What does?

MAISIE
 You.

MAX
 Well, that's because I'm an unrealistic person.

MAISIE
 But you shouldn't be! Seriously—who reads poetry?!

MAX

I do.

MAISIE

Well, can you stop?!

MAX

You're upset—

> *MAISIE gets up and turns off the gas.*

MAISIE

(from the stove)
You think I'm upset?

> *She pours hot water over the tea and sits back down, her hands wrapped around a mug.*

MAX

Let me rephrase: I know you're upset.

MAISIE

Stop knowing things about me, it's rude.

MAX

Ok.

MAISIE

How do you know things about me anyway? And why aren't you trying to flatter me more? Don't you want to be invited back?

MAX

You don't like to be flattered.

MAISIE

I'd still like you to try.

MAX

I want to see you again, Maisie.

MAISIE

I'm not sure why—

MAX

Because I like you.

MAISIE

I'm not sure why—

MAX

Because I just do. I mean who cares?

MAISIE

Say something reassuring!

MAX

I just did!

MAISIE

You think 'who cares' is reassuring!?

MAX

Sure. It's like saying: there's nothing to worry about.

MAISIE

There's everything to worry about! Are you crazy?!
You must be crazy—

MAX

You must be paranoid!

MAISIE

Can you be nice, please?

MAX

I'm trying—

MAISIE

Well it isn't working.

MAX

Why don't you read another poem?

MAISIE

No!—we're going to wake my roommate up; we're being too loud.

MAX

Read softly. Quietness is part of the meaning anyway.

MAISIE

The more you talk about meaningful things the more I'm going to wish that you weren't here.

MAX

I see.

MAISIE

Do you want me to make some coffee?

MAX

No, I'm alright, thanks.

MAISIE

Maybe you should pretend you're late for work or something; I feel awkward.

MAX

Why do you feel awkward?

MAISIE

Don't ask me questions you know I'm going to refuse to answer.

MAX

How do I know what questions you're going to refuse to answer?

MAISIE

Because I'm going to refuse to answer all of them.

MAX

Oh.

MAISIE

Are you really surprised that I'm being like this?

MAX

I don't know. I'm trying not to have expectations.

MAISIE

That's good.

MAX

Why is it good?

MAISIE

Because expectations are like helium balloons: they want to fly away.

MAX

Maybe you're afraid of your own expectations—

MAISIE

Maybe.

MAX

Maisie—

MAISIE

What?!

MAX

Look at me—

MAISIE

I don't want to.

MAX

Just look at me for a quick second, ok?

MAISIE

Ok.

MAX

Ok, so this is intense for me too. Like, I agree: it's scary to meet someone out of the blue. But I don't want this to end. I don't want to go home. I don't want to be on the subway reading a book, checking my phone every seven seconds to see if you've messaged me...and I know, um, I will be—pretty soon, actually—but the point is, I'm going to want to see you again—and I don't care if you're completely nuts—which you are, by the way—I just know that this feeling of weightlessness that I have right now is unique to the experience of having met you, and that I don't want to let it dissipate as if it was never there—

MAISIE

I like that you're emotional.

MAX

Are you sure about that?

MAISIE

No.

MAX

That's what I thought.

MAISIE

What are you thinking about?

MAX

Nothing.

MAISIE

Tell me.

MAX

It's just that I know that you're not going to break up with what's-his-name—

MAISIE

David—

MAX

Right, that you're not going to break up with David.

MAISIE

I thought you said there was nothing to worry about right now.

MAX

Well, I was full of shit. There's a lot to worry about.

MAISIE

Max—

MAX

What?

MAISIE

I got carried away by the moment—*ok?*—and now I don't know what to do. Do you understand that? *Max*—I'm serious—don't roll your eyes.

MAX

I'm not rolling my eyes.

MAISIE

Yes you are!

MAX

If you don't like my reactions, why don't you look somewhere else when you're talking to me!

MAISIE

Now you're mad at me.

MAX

I'm not mad at you. I just know how these things go. After I leave, I'm never going to hear from you again.

MAISIE

No, I promise you will.

MAX

I'm not counting on it.

MAISIE

Max—

MAX

What?!

MAISIE

Why are you looking at me like that? You're acting like it's the end of the world.

MAX

I just hate trying to not feel astonished when I wake up with someone I care about—

MAISIE

Max, that's very beautiful, and you can feel whatever you want to feel, but it's not that simple for me—

MAX

Maisie—why are you pretending to be so ambivalent!?

MAISIE

Maybe because I'm *actually* ambivalent—

MAX

Or maybe because you don't have the courage to be certain about someone you're not 'in a relationship with'.

MAISIE

Courage is overrated.

MAX

No, actually, I think it's extremely underrated—

MAISIE

Can you just be patient with me? Please?

MAX

I can try.

MAISIE

Because I really like you—

MAX

Well, I like you too—

MAISIE

But liking you is so intense...can't you be less romantic and more funny? I would really like that.

MAX

I think I'm funny.

MAISIE

But not that kind of funny.

MAX

What kind of funny?

MAISIE

The stupid, easy to write off kind.

MAX

Oh.

MAISIE

I just wanna know what your trick is.

MAX

There's no trick.

MAISIE

But I feel like I'm being tricked—

MAX

That's not my problem.

MAISIE

I'm just so not used to not being alone inside my head. I'm not used to someone else milling around, opening up all the drawers, looking through old letters and photographs...

MAX

Isn't that what empathy is?

MAISIE

No, that's what voyeurism is.

MAX

Trying to understand someone? Asking them questions? Suggesting new ways of thinking about things?

MAISIE

Well why is it so important for you to understand me? It feels frankly, a bit sterile and technical and just off…like, I'm not that complicated! I play the viola, I like living by myself; I like the warmth of my teacup when I pick it up in the morning. I like poetry…I even like reading it to you. *Why are you pouting?*

MAX

Because you say you don't want to be understood and that there's nothing that complicated to understand, but there's a reason that last night happened; you know?—like if your relationship with David, or whatever-his-name-is, was going well, there wouldn't be room for me; like you wouldn't have kept talking to me, or asked me to get coffee with you, or asked me to come up with you; none of that would have happened if there wasn't some need already there, some desire to be with someone else.

MAISIE

Oh, stop acting like you know everything about me! You didn't even realize that I already owned the book you gave me! I hid my copy under my bed last night so you wouldn't see it…of course I read poetry you idiot!

MAX

I see…

MAISIE

And what really bothers me, is that in your mind, you probably thought you were giving me a cultural education…gimme me a fucking break—

MAX

I thought you were trying to be quiet—

MAX looks up:

Enter EMILY, holding a smartphone and a water-bottle.

EMILY sits down at the table and looks at MAX.

EMILY

I'm Emily, Maisie's roommate.

Max sticks out his hand.

MAX

Max.

EMILY

(not taking his hand)
Hi there.

EMILY turns towards MAISIE.

EMILY (cont'd)

Good morning, princess.

MAISIE

Morning.

> *EMILY takes a sip from her water-bottle and scrolls through her phone.*

> *MAX gets up.*

MAX

Anyway, I've gotta go…I'll cya later Maisie.

> *MAISIE looks at him uncertainly, biting her lip.*

> *MAX stops in the doorway.*

MAISIE

Text me—

MAX

Ok, I'll text you.

> *MAX looks at MAISIE from the doorway.*

MAX

It was nice meeting you Emily.

EMILY

Cya.

> *Exit MAX.*

EMILY (cont'd)

A friend of yours?

MAISIE
I don't wanna talk about it.

EMILY
Oh yes you do.

MAISIE
It's not important.

EMILY
You fucked him—

MAISIE
It's not important.

EMILY
You fucked him—

MAISIE
Maybe.

EMILY
And?

MAISIE
I don't wanna talk about it.

EMILY
Ok.

MAISIE
I'm being ridiculous—

EMILY
No, I would be the same way.

MAISIE
Would you?

EMILY
What happened Maisie?

MAISIE
It's complicated.

EMILY
No, I'm guessing it's really not.

MAISIE
I was feeling stressed, or vulnerable, or something...I don't know! He was charming!

EMILY
He seemed upset when I came in.

MAISIE
Because I was being mean to him—

EMILY
Do you think you'll see him again?

MAISIE
No.

EMILY
Why not?

MAISIE
  Because, I'm with David.

EMILY
  But you like this guy, right?

MAISIE
  Yes, I like him *way* too much.

EMILY
  Then see him again—

MAISIE
  I'm with David.

EMILY
  So you don't want a mistress?—

MAISIE
  No. I'm not really the type.

EMILY
    (while looking at her phone)
  Are you happy with David?

MAISIE
  I guess.

EMILY
  Be honest—

MAISIE
  Well I'm a little out of it right now, ok?—this was a really new experience for me—

EMILY

Yeah, it's called an orgasm.

EMILY receives a text message and picks up her phone.

MAISIE

You didn't just text David, did you?

EMILY

Why would I text David?

MAISIE

I don't know why I said that. I'm sorry.

EMILY

It's just a strange thing to accuse me of.

MAISIE

It wasn't an accusation: it was just a reaction.

EMILY

A reaction to what?

MAISIE

I don't know! To guilt? To having done something wrong?

EMILY

Ok, whatever, I get it…are you going to tell David?

MAISIE

No.

EMILY

He would freak out?

MAISIE

Yes, he would freak out.

EMILY

He would break up with you?

MAISIE

Yes.

EMILY

And wouldn't that be preferable to having to pretend that he makes you happy?

MAISIE

These questions are making me nervous.

EMILY

I noticed.

MAISIE

Do you think David would break up me?

EMILY

Probably.

MAISIE

How would you know?

EMILY

Because he just would.

MAISIE

What do you mean!? you're being so vague!

EMILY

David would break up with you to avoid a conflict;
that's all.

MAISIE

What do you mean?

EMILY

I mean, David takes the path of least resistance. It's
one of his more obvious faults.

MAISIE

What obvious faults!?

EMILY

Maisie, don't be a fool—

MAISIE

You're trapping me—

EMILY

You're trapping yourself.

MAISIE

I *hate* that he's obvious.

EMILY

I didn't say he was obvious.

MAISIE

But you might as well have—

EMILY

But I didn't—

MAISIE

I know how hyper-intuitive you are Emily, ok? You don't have to show off—

EMILY

I'm not showing off.

MAISIE

Then what are you doing?

EMILY

Refereeing the little game you've set up here.

MAISIE

What game?

EMILY

Confession and penitence—

MAISIE

Oh.

EMILY

So, go on: confess—

MAISIE

I don't want to—

EMILY

Oh, yes you do.

MAISIE

Last night, space and time folded up; and I felt like I
was set in motion—

EMILY

Do you feel 'in-motion' with David?

MAISIE

No, I feel completely still.

EMILY

Uhuh.

MAISIE

It's like you're accusing me of something—

EMILY

Maisie, why are you with someone who bores you?

MAISIE

I don't know? Why is *anyone* with *anyone*!?

EMILY

You tell me!

MAISIE

Well, you asked!

EMILY

Well, you wanted to be asked.

MAISIE

You think I'm lying to myself!

EMILY

You're the one who's with someone you don't love!

MAISIE

I didn't say that!

EMILY

You suggested it.

MAISIE

Yeah, but I don't know why I did! To feel anything—
anything—for Max is just so ridiculous right now...I
mean, like, how should I know that he that doesn't pick
someone up every time he sits down at a Starbucks...
like, he probably does! I probably was one of those
girls!—like, Emily: it shouldn't have been that easy
for him, and it *was—I was*...and what's worse is that
now I feel completely heartbroken over him and he's
barely been gone for ten damn seconds...and even
though I'm generally not in the business of being a
butterfly catcher, if someone doesn't give me a net
pretty soon, this room is gonna fill up with the pink
and yellow wings that are currently threatening to
burst from my abdomen—

EMILY

Idea: why don't you text him and tell him to come
back?

MAISIE

Because I don't trust him! I don't even know him!

And I don't *want to trust him*! I don't want to know him! That's the whole point!

EMILY

Why shouldn't it have been easy for him?

MAISIE

Can you forget I said that?

EMILY

You're just worried that he thinks you're slut.

MAISIE

Yes! Because he probably does!

EMILY

Maisie, no one thinks you're a slut.

MAISIE

But I still feel like Max does.

EMILY

But he doesn't.

MAISIE

Ok, but—

EMILY

But what?

MAISIE

I'm still upset.

EMILY

And I'm still waiting for you to stop b-s'ing yourself.

MAISIE

Can you me a break Emily? You jump on everything I
say with some kind of...*remark*...and it's not helping!

EMILY

Well how can I best help you, then, Maisie?

MAISIE

By letting me contradict myself for a second—ok?
Because I know the contradictions are there, I can
hear myself. I know I'm vacillating and self-defeating
and blah blah blah. It's just like...I don't even know
why I woke up so early, because I barely slept...I don't
know why I don't feel tired...I should be exhausted,
but I'm not: I'm completely awake...

EMILY

And why do you think you feel so miraculously
awake?

MAISIE

You're asking me so many questions...

EMILY

You keep answering them.

MAISIE

You're not even paying attention to what I'm saying,
you've been on your phone half the time.

EMILY puts down her phone.

EMILY

So what?

MAISIE

So what? *It's rude!*

EMILY

Well then, I apologize.

MAISIE

No, I'm sorry, I'm being unfair.

EMILY

Yes you are.

MAISIE

I just don't like how composed you are.

EMILY

Neither do I.

MAISIE

This is terrible.

EMILY

What is?

MAISIE

Being so emotional. Or...I don't know!—just feeling like a lighthouse that can't shut off its search-light once the storm's passed...I've got, like, no self-healing mechanism, just wound after wound after wound after wound—

EMILY

(stroking Maisie's hair)
Oh, but you're so pretty Maisie!

MAISIE

What the fuck is wrong you with you Emily!

EMILY

Geeze, relax. I'm just teasing you.

MAISIE

You're making me feel so childish!

EMILY

What's wrong with feeling childish?

MAISIE

What is with the questions Emily?! I feel like you're interrogating me!

EMILY

I told you: it's fun.

MAISIE

I'm not here to amuse you!

EMILY

And yet, you're amusing me anyway.

MAISIE

Can you just go back to bed? I don't feel like being made fun of.

EMILY

Maisie, you obviously need someone to talk to—I'm serious—so I'm here; I'm listening. Just ignore my side comments—

MAISIE

I don't see how I can.

EMILY

You're upset, I get it—

MAISIE

No! I'm not just 'upset'—I'm genuinely beginning to question some things right now that I've believed for a long time, or thought I believed...and the idea that you can feel how weak I am right now and are exploiting it for your own entertainment—

EMILY

I don't think you're weak—

MAISIE

Yes you do: it's like we're both walking through a desert, but only you have water—

EMILY

No...

EMILY gets up and goes to the sink, where she fills up a glass of water and puts it to MAISIE'S lips:

EMILY (cont'd)

...we're in an apartment where we both have water
from the tap.

MAISIE

It's not funny.

EMILY

What's not funny?

MAISIE

How much power you have over me!

EMILY

You're crazy.

MAISIE

I'm beginning to feel like it.

> *MAISIE gets up abruptly and takes a bottle of
> whiskey out of the cabinet and pours it into her
> tea and returns back to the table.*

MAISIE (cont'd)

I'm sorry if I woke you up this morning.

EMILY

You *did* wake me up.

MAISIE

And now I need a drink and I don't think it's even
9:00 clock yet.

EMILY

It's 9:30.

MAISIE

Well then I'm perfectly justified, I think, in temporarily suspending my standards for daytime sobriety.

EMILY looks at her phone.

MAISIE (cont'd)

Please don't look at your phone Emily—

EMILY

Sorry, I got a text.

MAISIE

This early?

EMILY

Jesus—

MAISIE

I'm sorry.

EMILY

You're so paranoid!

MAISIE

That's what Max said.

EMILY

I just don't get it.

MAISIE

You're angry with me—

EMILY

I wish I was. That would be easier.

MAISIE

I don't know what that means.

EMILY

Does that bother you?

MAISIE

Yes! I want to understand you Emily! I want us to be friends!

EMILY laughs.

MAISIE (cont'd)

Why are you laughing!

EMILY

Never mind.

EMILY picks up her phone.

MAISIE

Emily—

EMILY

Maisie: if you're going to act like a moody child, I'm not going to give you the courtesy of my attention; I'm really not.

MAISIE

Fair enough.

EMILY

Thank you—

EMILY goes back to texting.

MAISIE

Do you ever feel like maybe people don't *actually* need to feel alone all the time? Do you think that's possible?

EMILY

(texting)

No. I feel alone all the time. I'm over it. Whatever.

MAISIE raises her eyebrows and looks directly at EMILY, who doesn't meet her gaze.

MAISIE

Then what are you doing here Emily?

EMILY

Whatd'ya mean?

MAISIE

I mean in New York—or in this room, anywhere? I mean...why aren't you doing something about that feeling?

EMILY

Because why waste my time?!

MAISIE

Because it's depressing to give up!

EMILY

No, it's trying too hard that's depressing.

MAISIE

No! That's terrible! I refuse to believe that loneliness is just something that a person has to accept, like aging or death or something—

EMILY

No, that's exactly what loneliness is. People don't change Maisie. It's that simple. Loneliness, aging death, in that order. That's life. You are what you are. I am what I am. Then we die.

MAISIE

What does that even mean, Emily?

EMILY

It means you don't call A 'B' and B 'A'.

MAISIE

So what am I? An 'A' and you're a 'B'.

EMILY

(putting down her phone)
Something like that.

MAISIE

And what does my letter stand for?

EMILY

Innocence.

MAISIE

I'm not innocent.

EMILY

If you weren't innocent, you wouldn't be upset right now—

MAISIE

You are so condescending to me—

EMILY

No, Maisie, I envy you.

MAISIE

But you think I'm a child!

EMILY

Yes exactly—and who doesn't envy a child?

MAISIE

I don't!

EMILY

Why?

MAISIE

Why?…because children are *so incredibly alone, Emily*. That's what childhood is. We're taught right away how alone we are, and then we're taught it again and again and again…and that's why it's so incredibly terrifying to wake up with someone and not feel like it's not some kind of inexcusable error…to not feel lonely all of a sudden…because it goes against what we've been taught is possible…I mean God, Emily, I was so happy to grow up and stop being a kid, because it meant I could quit music school, and get a regular job, and because I could begin the process of not just doing what I'm told…and even though I'm still not sure how to live if I'm not pleasing my parents or my instructors or someone, someone— you, David, Beethoven, Bach; someone—I'm still relieved to just be a regular old lonely adult, and not an extraordinarily alone child anymore—

EMILY

OK—I get it—

MAISIE

But then again, you probably have no idea how I felt when I was a kid! Because Emily, I don't think that you know how it feels to get close to something great—which is what music can be—and to not have anyone to share that feeling with: not your parents, who are more concerned about themselves than you, not your peers, who are jealous beyond belief, and not your friends who are complete, *fucking philistines;* no you have no idea how isolating it is to be moved by something that beautiful—because you can fuck whomever you want, and paint whatever you want, and not feel like you're betraying anything beautiful

or sacred or divine, and...don't just look at your
phone, *my fucking God Emily!*

EMILY

Why should I listen to you tell me that I'm some kind
of some kind of emotionless bitch?

MAISIE

Oh no! I'm sorry! You're not! You're supposed to stop
me from saying things like that! You shouldn't take
me literally.

EMILY

Oh! But I just was beginning to enjoy the bit about
having never touched greatness—

MAISIE

Emily—

EMILY

What?

MAISIE

I don't dislike you, you know.

EMILY

That's reassuring.

MAISIE

Well what else should I say?

EMILY

You should just say that my presence is oppressive.

That I 'don't get you' and 'don't do the dishes' and make too much noise when I have sex.

MAISIE

Emily, what are you talking about?

EMILY

I'm saying: *throw some roommate cliches at me! Belittle me.* Isn't that what people are supposed to do in this situation?!

MAISIE

Why should I care about what people are supposed to do?

EMILY

Because!

MAISIE

Because what?

EMILY

Because cliches are the best thing you can ever throw at an argument—it makes the conflict evaporate into an ether of pure banality—

MAISIE

This isn't an argument, there's *no* conflict.

EMILY

There's conflict.

MAISIE

No, I refuse to admit it. I shouldn't have said anything to you.

MAISIE stands up.

MAISIE (cont'd)

Do you want me to make breakfast? I could make eggs!

EMILY

Hatred unites people Maisie. Not friendship, not love, not pity.

MAISIE sits down again.

EMILY (cont'd)

Do you think I'm kidding?

MAISIE

No. I think you're completely serious.

EMILY

That's right: I am.

MAISIE

You know I fell in love last night?—right?—and that I just couldn't admit it to him, or to myself? That I was just lying in bed…you know, after we did it— after we *fucked*—feeling like someone had suddenly thrown aside a curtain in a dark room—

EMILY

Maisie: of course you fell in love!

MAISIE

You're impossible to talk to!

EMILY

You woke up to play the viola at sunrise for God's sake.

MAISIE

That's true—

EMILY

It's too cheesy for it to be anything else—

MAISIE

But I don't like falling in love; its unmerited on all sides, and it's always so detrimental to self-control, which I consider to be critically important to the general problem of my always being on the verge of losing my shit—

EMILY

And don't forget that it means telling David that he was just keeping the boyfriend-seat warm while you successfully completed the search for someone with whom you share actual, human feelings.

MAISIE

It would be nice if once in a while you could just say

'you're absolutely right Maisie, and I have no further comments'.

EMILY
   (nodding)
You're absolutely right Maisie, and I have no further comments.

MAISIE
   Emily!

EMILY
   I only did what you asked.

MAISIE
   Can you please just not put me down all the time though? I mean, you're so smart Emily; you're so beautiful...you don't need to prove that I'm a less impressive person than you are, because it's already obvious that I'm not; that I'm just the girl whose attempts to re-enter the sunshine each morning are complicated by the overwhelming desire to dive back into bed and hide under the covers...

EMILY
   Do you really think I'm any different? Honestly—

MAISIE
   I like to pretend that you are.

EMILY
   I'm not.

MAISIE

Emily...maybe *you* should sleep with Max!

EMILY

Maisie—

MAISIE

That would make things so much easier!...don't look at me like I'm crazy!

EMILY

Well, you are crazy!

MAISIE

Don't you think that you and Max would get along? I wouldn't be hurt...I'd be relieved!

EMILY

You'd be hurt. Trust me.

MAISIE

No!—it makes *so* much sense!

EMILY

Maisie—you would be hurt.

MAISIE

Who cares! I'd rather be hurt than hurt David.

EMILY

Oh Maisie, who gives a fuck about David? And besides, you won't hurt him, because he's not the kind of person who gets hurt.

MAISIE

How can you say that?

EMILY

Because he's just not—

MAISIE

You say that with such certainty.

EMILY

Ok. Interpret as you will.

MAISIE

Emily: there's something you're not telling me.

EMILY

Like what?

MAISIE

I don't know!? Do you talk to David? Does he tell you things about me?

EMILY

I see David on his way to your room Maisie, and on his way back out. That's it.

MAISIE

Then how do you know things about him?

EMILY

I told you: it's a guess.

MAISIE

Based on what?

EMILY

Context.

MAISIE

What context?

EMILY

You, Maisie. What you say. How you talk about him.
How you seem right before he arrives and right after
he leaves.

MAISIE

And how's that? how do I seem?

EMILY

Impatient to be alone again.

MAISIE

That's true...I mean, I guess there's a reason I told
him I didn't want to live together.

EMILY

Well there ya go.

MAISIE

But I don't like imagining myself like that, like
someone disinterested in their own relationship.

EMILY

Then don't imagine it.

MAISIE

You're making me imagine it.

EMILY

Well let's talk about Max then, instead.

MAISIE

What is there to say?

EMILY

To begin with, you didn't seem disinterested in him when I came in here. In fact, you seemed very interested.

MAISIE

I was.

EMILY

Go on—

MAISIE

I don't know! He held my hand on the way up the stairs. He didn't talk about himself very much. He asked me questions. He knew about music and he wasn't bullshitting. So I was interested; like, very interested...*I pursued him.* I approached him, I asked him if he wanted to go somewhere else and talk. I've never ever done that. I'll probably never ever do that again. It was a one-time thing. Which is the point! That it was an accident, or like: something I needed to prove to myself—

EMILY

What did you need to prove to yourself?

MAISIE

That I could actually let myself be moved by another
human being…God, this sounds horrible, I'm sorry—
it must sound so horrible—

EMILY

It didn't sound horrible.

MAISIE

What did it sound like then?

EMILY

It sounded true.

MAISIE

Oh, yeah—right.

EMILY

But maybe you don't like the sound of 'true'—

MAISIE

No, I don't.

EMILY

Maybe you should.

MAISIE

I feel like you're judging me.

EMILY

No, not really.

MAISIE

Yes you are. I mean, I would judge me, Emily.

EMILY

What would I judge you for? For sleeping with someone who wasn't your boyfriend?

MAISIE

No, for not knowing myself at all.

EMILY

Maisie, I think that you *do* know yourself, you just don't want to do anything about it...if I'm judging you for anything, it's that—

MAISIE

Not 'doing something'—

EMILY

Yes.

MAISIE

And what am I 'not doing'?

EMILY

Breaking up with David.

MAISIE

What would that accomplish?

EMILY

Well, for starters, you wouldn't feel guilt about acting on a simple desire!

MAISIE

There's no such thing as a simple desire!

EMILY

Only if you decide to rationalize every fucking thing you do Maisie!

MAISIE

Do you really think that I should break up with David?

EMILY

Yes—

MAISIE

I'm afraid of doing something I'll regret…

EMILY

What would you possibly regret?

MAISIE

Being alone.

EMILY

But you are alone. *You're alone inside of your relationship*—

MAISIE

That doesn't mean I won't regret being outside of it—

EMILY

Maisie: have you ever thought that if you're bored, he's also bored?

MAISIE

I'm not bored though. I mean. It isn't boring with David. Not exactly. It's *something*, sure, but not that…

rolling around naked on the bed like dry fish...there's something more than habitual affection; there's really poetry in our attempt; in the tenderness of failing...I don't know, I don't know. Maybe that's ridiculous. I just can't stand to be honest with myself, Emily...I just can't...it's terrible—

EMILY

That sounded honest.

MAISIE

But how can I really be honest with David?

EMILY

By calling him up and going, 'Hey Dave, I fucked some random guy, anyway, it's over, bye'—just like that.

MAISIE

Oh that's *really* useful advice—

EMILY

Why isn't it?

MAISIE

Because I could never be that cold to someone.

EMILY

Why not?

MAISIE

What do you have against David? You're acting like he's some kind of terrible person—

EMILY

You don't know that he isn't—

MAISIE

Emily! What the fuck! You don't know him! That's so unfair! He's someone I care about!

EMILY

Fine. I retract my last statement.

MAISIE

What do you think I should tell him?

EMILY

I have no idea Maisie.

MAISIE

I want to know what you think!

EMILY

I think you should just do whatever you want to do, ok? If I say anything else you'll just freak out—

MAISIE

But I don't just want to do whatever I want. It would feel so selfish...

EMILY

What's wrong with that?

MAISIE

What are you saying?

EMILY

I'm saying, Maisie, that it might feel good to quote 'be selfish'.

MAISIE

No, I don't agree at all! I like the idea of giving unconditionally to someone else...*I like the idea of not wanting anything!*

EMILY

But you do want things! That's my point! You'll always want things. Everybody wants things. And in subtle ways Maisie, if you really think about yourself, you'll find that you're just as selfish as everybody else... as I am, as David is, as Max is...that you take the same way that everybody else does: which is without asking first.

MAISIE

Don't you think that there's some kind of real goodness in people?

EMILY

Not really, no.

MAISIE

Because I do. It's there in people, like sheet-music that hasn't been played—

EMILY

The only thing inside of people is hunger.

MAISIE

Probably.

EMILY

That's not what you wanted to hear—

MAISIE

Why do you reflexively reject every kind of higher ideal in life? I want to know—

EMILY

Because they don't exist! I mean, look at you Maisie: you're just hiding behind the idea of commitment because you're afraid to be alone!

MAISIE

And you're pretending you don't care about anything so that I don't notice that you're just as vulnerable as I am—

EMILY

Thank you captain-fucking-obvious!

MAISIE

So can you stop acting like you've got your shit figured out! Because you don't! Neither of us does—

EMILY

I'm not pretending to have my shit figured out, I'm asking you to stop being so naive about people.

MAISIE

How am I naive about people?

EMILY

You think we've all just to make an extra-special promise not to lie to each other and everything will be fine; it's just like: be realistic, kid—promises are a sign that desperation has already set in, that we're already deep inside the lie itself.

MAISIE

Did someone really hurt you Emily? I feel like you're talking about something that happened to you—

EMILY

No, that's exactly my point: nothing special happened to me—I'm just describing what I see around me. Table, chair, self-deception, and so on. Building, car, cheater, conman, liar, asshole.

MAISIE

There's something about you this morning Emily, that's making me really uncomfortable.

EMILY

Good. I'm glad you're uncomfortable.

MAISIE

What I don't understand is why you resent me so much.

EMILY

It's simple: because you resent me.

MAISIE
  What?!

EMILY
  I know: *shocking*.

MAISIE
  I don't resent you at all! I honestly think that you're
  trying to help me!

EMILY
  No, that's just what you're telling yourself—

MAISIE
  Then what are you doing?

EMILY
  Pulling the pin out—

MAISIE
  I don't understand—

EMILY
  So that you fall apart—

MAISIE
  Did I do something to you Emily?

EMILY
  No you haven't. Which is the problem.

MAISIE
  I don't understand...

EMILY

And you don't need to.

MAISIE

You're so physically beautiful Emily, you know that; but you repel people, and you know that too...

EMILY

What does being beautiful have to do with any of this?

MAISIE

It's like you don't like there to be anything else bright while you're in the same room...you don't want there to be any other source of light...like, even though you say otherwise, you like getting what you want... you say you don't like it, but you would never, *never* want to be weaker or less beautiful than you are! And you don't want anyone to challenge you! I feel like you're secretly terrified of the idea that someone could challenge you!

EMILY

Maybe.

MAISIE

And...I look at your art; you know—your paintings— and I think that you must be the most intricately frail person on earth...like the tiny little mint plant we have on the windowsill, desperate for those few hours every day when the sunlight pours through the glass…and I get how the economy of sunlight works because I need it too, Emily—the sunlight I mean—but the way you randomly wound people just to build up your own strength…that's something that I refuse to do…it's one thing to make it your prerogative to protect yourself; but at the cost of other people, of someone else—

EMILY picks up her phone.

EMILY

Uhuh, please continue—

MAISIE

I feel drunk…I'm sorry!

EMILY

That's because you've been drinking.

MAISIE pours more whiskey into her tea.

MAISIE

I offended you! I'm sorry!

EMILY

I'm not offended.

MAISIE

Yes you are. And it's so unjustified really; when I absolutely deserve to be mocked and criticized and God knows what else for what I've done to David.

EMILY

I still don't know why you're so concerned with David.

MAISIE

Because he really loves me—

EMILY

David doesn't love you.

MAISIE

Don't say that!

EMILY

But he doesn't—

MAISIE

I don't want to talk to you anymore. Can you go back to bed? Please?

EMILY

If you really believed David loved you, you wouldn't have slept with this other dude—Max—

MAISIE

Ok, maybe, yes, that's true…but what does it matter whether I admit it or not?…because I like the reassurance of saying, 'David loves me, David loves me,' over and over, even if I know that it's perniciously untrue…David's very good at being my boyfriend; and I like that. And up until last night, I was very good at being his girlfriend, which I also liked. Because I was marvelous, really really marvelous, at it…and now I've lost that: that self-satisfaction…I gave it away for free, despite how precious and how depleted my sources of self-satisfaction really are…I just hate—*hate*—the pretense of being an adult who has to preserve and protect themselves, just like I hated being a child who had to be vulnerable to everyone; I've always just wanted to be myself; somewhere in the middle of vulnerable and safe; or somewhere else altogether. Or just alone; by myself; where no one can ever ask too much of me...

EMILY

Maisie—

MAISIE

What?

EMILY

Everyone feels like too much is asked of them. You're describing everyone. No one feels like they are allowed to be themselves. *No one.* You're not even remotely special. You're suffering is not even remotely unique.

MAISIE

I should just shut up.

> *EMILY smiles slightly and takes a sip of MAISIE'S tea.*

EMILY

I'm going back to sleep.

MAISIE

Can you tell me if I offended you? please?

EMILY

You didn't offend me Maisie, I told you already.

Exit EMILY.

MAISIE reaches for the book, still on the table. Exit MAISIE, carrying the book.

Cue: The sound of MAISIE practicing the viola.

Stage goes dark.

Music stops.

Cue: sound of door shutting, someone walking down a set of stairs, a second door shutting a floor below.

ACT II

Lights brighten.

EMILY is on the futon, looking at her phone.

Enter DAVID, who lets himself in.

DAVID

Emily…is Maisie here?

EMILY

You just missed her.

DAVID sits down on the futon and seems to relax.

DAVID

How long is she going to be gone?

EMILY

I think it's a safe bet that she won't be back for a few hours.

DAVID

Are you sure?

EMILY

Yes.

DAVID

That's good, because I want to talk to you—

EMILY

Of course you do.

DAVID

Yes, because this is not an easy situation—

EMILY shrugs indifferently.

DAVID
Why did you text me this morning? I didn't need to know that she slept with someone else—

EMILY
I thought you'd be glad to know we're off the hook—

DAVID
We're not off the hook.

EMILY
Well everyone is even now, right? Morally speaking—

DAVID
Maisie and I are far from even.

EMILY
Oh, but she's really made up a lot of lost ground!

DAVID
Yeah! And there's a lot more ground to make up! Months and months of lost ground...

DAVID gets up from the futon and begins to pace.

DAVID
I don't know how you can be so calm!

EMILY
Trust me, I'm not calm.

DAVID
You look calm!

EMILY

Looks can be deceiving.

DAVID

What are you thinking?

EMILY

Nothing.

DAVID

What are you feeling?

EMILY

Nothing.

DAVID

Why are you lying to me?

EMILY

I'm not lying to you.

DAVID

Then what are you doing?

EMILY

Nothing.

DAVID

I feel like you're going to tell Maisie about us—

EMILY

She's not going to find out.

DAVID

How do you know?

EMILY

Because she is stupid enough to trust you and not me.

DAVID

I feel terrible...

EMILY

Not so terrible that you want to stop sleeping with me.

DAVID shakes his head passively, not making eye-contact with EMILY.

EMILY

You are a wonderful performer.

DAVID

I'm not performing, I'm disintegrating.

EMILY

Same thing.

DAVID

When did Maisie leave?

EMILY

Maybe an hour ago.

DAVID

Where did she go?

EMILY

Who knows.

DAVID sits back down and puts his hand on EMILY'S inner thigh.

DAVID
Can you kiss me—please?

EMILY
Absolutely not.

DAVID
Why?

EMILY
Because I'm not doing that anymore.

DAVID
Doing what?

EMILY
That.

DAVID
Why not?

EMILY
Because it gives me bad dreams.

DAVID
What does that mean?

EMILY
It means *no*.

DAVID
Kiss me.

EMILY
No!

DAVID

I want to make love to you.

EMILY

You don't make love: you make yourself happy.

DAVID

Emily—

EMILY

What?

DAVID

Why did you say that?

EMILY

Do you ever hear yourself when you speak?

DAVID

I don't understand—what are you trying to say?

EMILY

I'm just wondering—

DAVID

Everyone hears themselves speak! I don't know! Yes? No? what does it fucking matter?

EMILY

What I want to know is…how far do your words sink into you before they're buoyed back up to the surface?

DAVID

Far enough.

EMILY

Because I forced your girlfriend to listen to herself this morning, and I'm not sure why, but I *did*—and I liked it. And now I want to do the same thing to you: I wanna make you listen to yourself—I don't want to let you just avoid…and avoid…and avoid…

DAVID

Why are you telling me this?

EMILY

Because it's important.

DAVID

You're warning me about something…

EMILY

Yes, that's right: I am.

> *DAVID sits up on the futon and looks squarely at EMILY.*

DAVID

I'm aware of who you are, Emily.

EMILY

What does *that* mean?

DAVID

It means that I recognize you for what you are.

EMILY

And *what* am I?

DAVID

Exactly what I am.

EMILY

Which is *what*, David?

DAVID

Someone who betrays, someone who is unfaithful.

EMILY

Oh, that is *so* dramatic!

DAVID

You don't think that *this* is dramatic?

EMILY

No, I don't.

DAVID

Why?

EMILY

Because I don't take myself that seriously—

DAVID

Maybe you should.

EMILY

Maybe, maybe, maybe: you and Maisie have the same favorite word.

DAVID

Kiss me.

> *EMILY pushes him away.*

EMILY

Fuck off David.

DAVID touches EMILY'S ankle.

EMILY

I said fuck off!

DAVID recoils.

DAVID

Alright, Jesus.

EMILY puts her phone down and sits up.

EMILY

Do you love me? I want you to tell me.

DAVID shrugs.

EMILY

Answer me.

DAVID

I don't have an answer.

EMILY

You're not capable of one.

DAVID

That question doesn't have an answer, Emily—for anyone, ever.

EMILY

No, just for you it doesn't.

DAVID

What do you want me to say Emily?!

EMILY

I want you to say 'yes' or 'no'.

DAVID

Well I can't! I'm sorry!

EMILY

Yeah, you're sorry about everything, aren't you?

DAVID

Right now I am.

EMILY

It's just so incredibly *easy* to be sorry; that's what I can't get over. Why don't you do something difficult David? Oh wait, I know the answer: because it's easier to just do whatever the fuck you want and then just issue a tepid apology for it later!

DAVID

Look, given the circumstances—

EMILY

You fucking your girlfriend's roommate!

DAVID

Yes, ok, given *those* circumstances—

EMILY

You fucking your girlfriend's roommate—

DAVID

Yes, whatever, given *that*—

EMILY

Say it!

DAVID

Say what?

EMILY

Say what the circumstances are!

DAVID

Ok: given that *I'm fucking my girlfriend's roommate*—I'm...
no: I'm not going to say anything—

EMILY

You just can't bring yourself to say what it is you're actually
doing!? Can you?!

DAVID

Just leave me alone.

EMILY

I can't, because you're in the middle of my apartment—

DAVID

Why did you ask if I loved you?

> *EMILY picks her phone back up from the floor and
> lays back on the futon.*

EMILY

Because I wanted to see your reaction.

DAVID stands up.

DAVID

You're fucking crazy Emily.

EMILY

This morning I woke up and decided I wouldn't bullshit either of you anymore; you or Maisie. So I'm not. And it's great. You are both completely incapable of listening to someone tell you the truth.

DAVID sits back down.

DAVID

Why haven't you told Maisie about us yet?...I feel like you're just waiting for the most destructive moment possible—

EMILY

Because I am waiting for the most destructive moment possible—

DAVID

But you're involved in this too!—that's what I don't get! If you make things complicated for Maisie and I, you make things complicated for yourself too.

EMILY

Strictly speaking, David, that's correct.

DAVID

You're just as guilty as I am Emily!

EMILY

Guilt is like breathing or fucking or shitting to you David: it's all you're capable of.

DAVID

No, Emily, you're the one who's obsessed by guilt—

EMILY

Not guilt, shame. There's a difference. Guilt is being upset that someone caught you in the act. Shame is catching yourself.

DAVID

I think it's the other way around actually.

EMILY

Either way, there's an inescapable judgement—

DAVID

A judgement that you're always willing to affirm—

EMILY

The world is a strange and melancholy place, full of lonely, enigmatic people. And I'm one of them.

DAVID stands up.

DAVID

I'm gonna go.

EMILY bites her lower lip.

EMILY

Ciao.

DAVID goes to the door.

EMILY

David—

DAVID turns at the door.

DAVID

You're gonna say: 'don't go'.

EMILY

Don't go.

DAVID goes back to the futon.

DAVID

What can I possibly say to you right now that won't get my head bitten off?

EMILY

I just want you to stick around for a little while.

DAVID

Why?

EMILY

Why do you think?

DAVID

I honestly don't know.

EMILY

You should know—

DAVID
What am I supposed to be guessing!—this is ridiculous.

EMILY
You're supposed to guess the reason that I want you to stay.

DAVID
Because you're lonely.

EMILY
Oh—shut up.

DAVID
What?

EMILY
No cliches, please.

DAVID
Loneliness is a cliche?

EMILY
Yes, it's a cliche.

DAVID
Alright. Well that was my guess.

EMILY
It was a bad guess.

DAVID
It's not a cliche if it's true.

EMILY

It can't be true if it's a cliche David…because it's such a shallow way of describing me. 'Oh she's lonely and takes pills and has Daddy issues and has read too many sad books'. Maybe that's all literally true, but it doesn't *fucking mean anything*. It's like saying, 'She breathes air, she bleeds, she cries, she's a human being'.

DAVID

I don't know what to say to that.

EMILY

Yes, you fucking do.

DAVID

Emily—

EMILY

I hate you.

DAVID

Emily—

EMILY

Did you hear me? I said *I hate you.* I don't want to look at you. I feel like holding my breath until I pass out or you leave. One or the other.

EMILY holds her breath in an exaggerated fashion.

DAVID

EMILY!

EMILY continues to hold her breath.

DAVID
  EMILY!

    EMILY continues to hold her breath.

DAVID
  EMILY!

    *DAVID grabs her by the shoulders and pushes her
    against a wall, forcing the breath from EMILY'S
    lungs.*

    EMILY pushes him away.

EMILY
  My hero.

    DAVID doesn't answer.

EMILY
  What David? Did I hurt your feelings?

    *DAVID gets up and goes to the window at the side of
    the stage, which he opens as wide as possible. DAVID
    takes a cigarette and lighter out from his pocket.
    DAVID sits in the window sill and lights his cigarette.*

DAVID
  Maisie hates when I smoke inside.

EMILY
  Then don't smoke.

    DAVID exhales in EMILY'S direction:

DAVID

You know...you just use me for deviance...and then you act like I'm just this empty, pathetic little beetle scuttling across your life...but what's really true is that you want to prevent me from being anything else to you...you explain me away Emily; you explain my entire personality as a trick to get you to hook up with me...and maybe it is; but whatever...I don't give a fuck...I know I'm not some fucking abstraction—which is what you want me to be: an empty space that you can fill up with everything you hate about your own life. So here I am! Your caricature of wounded masculinity! Your disinterested fuckbuddy! At your service. Use me as you like! Treat me like I don't exist! Who cares! I'm your cartoon!—erase me whenever I get too problematic. Because that's the kind of artist you are, right Emily?—solipsistic, self-involved; indifferent to the inner-lives of the subjects you choose to represent—

EMILY gets up and approaches DAVID.

EMILY

I assume you're happy now—

DAVID

Happier than I was.

EMILY kisses David softly on the lips and steps back.

EMILY

Because that was a very satisfying explanation—you're right: *I'm* responsible for what you say and do; *I'm* the one who should feel bad, and really you're just a victim of *my* indifference. Right right right: because I'm incapable, as a person and a painter, of seeing the beauty in you—right. What else is there to say?

DAVID snuffs the cigarette on the windowsill and approaches EMILY on the futon.

DAVID

Let's go to your room.

EMILY

Aren't you afraid that Maisie will come back?

DAVID

No.

EMILY

I am.

DAVID

I'm tired of caring.

EMILY

You were tired a long time ago.

DAVID

What do you mean?

EMILY

You know what I mean.

DAVID

You act like I don't care about Maisie.

EMILY
No, you act like you don't care about Maisie.

DAVID
Because I care about you—

EMILY
Uhuh.

DAVID
You wanted me to be honest!

EMILY
That's not honest.

DAVID
Then what is it?

EMILY
A strategy.

DAVID
A strategy for what?!

EMILY
Don't talk to me.

DAVID
Answer my question—

EMILY
No.

DAVID
Explain it to me—

EMILY
   I refuse—

DAVID
   Emily—

EMILY
   It's just so obvious—

DAVID
   Not to me.

EMILY
   No, of course not.

DAVID
   I want you to kiss me again.

EMILY
   No: that was the last time.

DAVID
   No it wasn't.

EMILY
   How do you know?

DAVID
   Because you do this—

EMILY
   Do what?

DAVID
   Make false guarantees.

EMILY

You take me too literally.

*EMILY kisses DAVID again. DAVID receives the
kiss dispassionately and breaks away:*

DAVID

Let's go to your room. I want to make love.

EMILY

I asked you not to call it that.

DAVID

Kiss me again.

EMILY

No.

*DAVID sits down on the futon, EMILY gets up as he
sits down and walks to the center of the room, with
her back to him.*

DAVID

Why not?

EMILY whirls around:

EMILY

What's your obsession with getting to the panties stage of
this little encounter so quickly, huh?

DAVID

I just want to stop talking…

EMILY

Right, because you have nothing, *nothing* to say.

DAVID

You are so smug.

EMILY

No, I'm something else.

DAVID

And what's that?

EMILY

Defensive, wounded, unhappy; bitter, corrosive, disappointed.

> *DAVID stands up and approaches her:*

DAVID

I want to touch you—

EMILY

Fuck off.

> *DAVID tries to kiss her.*

EMILY

I SAID FUCK OFF DAVID! OK!?

DAVID

Whatever you want.

> *DAVID walks to the door.*

EMILY

Come back here immediately.

DAVID turns in the doorway to face her.

DAVID

What if Maisie walks in?

EMILY

Then I lose a roommate, and you lose someone who will fuck you out of loyalty.

DAVID

You think it's just out of loyalty?

EMILY

Oh, you think you're *so* seductive David.

DAVID

No, you thought I was seductive Emily—which is why we're having this conversation in the first place.

EMILY

I didn't think you were seductive. I didn't think you were anything.

DAVID

Oh that's not true: I remember how excited you were to get undressed the first time, I remember laying you across the bed, how your lips were parted like you were about to start singing—

EMILY

You are so satisified with yourself—

DAVID

Wouldn't you be?

EMILY

You're obscene.

DAVID

I'm being honest: wouldn't you be pleased with yourself if you were me, Emily?

EMILY

Are you really asking me that question?

DAVID

Are you really not going to answer it?

EMILY

I can't—it's not a real question, it's an obsene gesture. It's disgusting.

DAVID

No, what's disgusting is pretending that you're someone different than who you are in bed.

EMILY doesn't answer.

DAVID

Emily—

EMILY

Don't look at me like you've won.

DAVID

I don't think I've 'won' anything.

EMILY

Oh yes you do. Yes you do David.

DAVID

Are you crying?

EMILY

It's possible.

DAVID

This is exhausting.

EMILY

It's exhilarating.

DAVID

What's exhilarating about this?

EMILY

Letting myself be torn open, like a pearl from its shell.

DAVID

Look, Emily, I just want you to treat me with some kind of
basic respect; I haven't deserved any of this—

EMILY

You slept with me.

DAVID

We acted as partners!

EMILY

You don't know anything about sex. It's more shocking
than the sex itself…

DAVID

You came twice the last time we were together.

EMILY

That's *exactly* what someone like you would bring up: as if it were actually true.

DAVID

Oh! Don't pretend—

EMILY

What good is an orgasm David, when your emotions have no connection to the physical feeling of getting fucked?!

DAVID

I don't know—

EMILY

Fight back!! Don't just shake your head!!

DAVID

What do you mean fight back?

EMILY

I mean stop thinking of a way out of this: just stop me from being like this...*God*—I sound like Maisie!

DAVID

What are you talking about?

EMILY

I'm talking about literally everything.

DAVID

You're taking your own guilt over Maisie out on me.

EMILY

Yes, of course I am, but why aren't you taking your guilt over Maisie out on me?!

DAVID

I don't want to be psychoanalyzed anymore.

EMILY

It's not psychology, David, it's dissonance. It's the melody turning against itself in midair—

DAVID

You know, I would love to spend more time talking to you Emily—getting to know you—learning to care for you— but when I see you, you're the one who wants to make love right away—you're the one who doesn't want to talk about anything—

EMILY

What good would it do to get to know each other? It's impossible! David, I refuse, I just refuse to think of our quick, illicit fucks as some kind of soul-to-soul communion—

DAVID

See, you do this: you act like everything we do is too morally disgusting to be discussed—

EMILY

Yes, because words would mean collusion between my brain and the rest of my body!

DAVID

Why can't you just accept that I have feelings for you?

EMILY

Because you don't!

DAVID

Will you stop telling me what I feel!?

EMILY

When I stop knowing what you feel, I will stop telling you.

DAVID takes her hand.

DAVID

I love you Emily.

EMILY

Please don't use that word...

DAVID

But I do, I love you so much—

EMILY

You leave people just as lonely as they were when you found them.

DAVID lets go of her hand.

DAVID

You're trying to make me feel desperate. And I do. I feel incredibly desperate—

EMILY

Well good for you.

DAVID takes a phone out of his pocket and begins to scroll.

EMILY

Are you kidding me?

DAVID ignores her.

EMILY

I want you to show me an emotion—

DAVID

I did, and it wasn't good enough.

EMILY

David—

DAVID

No.

EMILY

I need you to look at me.

DAVID

No, sorry.

EMILY

I just want someone to breathe some life into me…I don't care how anymore…I really don't…I just need it.

DAVID puts his phone down.

DAVID

Then don't belittle the people around you.

EMILY

I'm not belittling you, David, I'm fighting against you.

DAVID

I don't fight.

EMILY

I know. You want to retain the ultimate privilege of not having to mean what you say—and you're struggling to not be provoked into it—into meaning; because, like—

DAVID

Just stop just stop just stop—

EMILY

I can't.

DAVID

You're making noise—

EMILY

You can't hear the melody, then; it's very very very soft—

DAVID

I feel a kind of tension here—

DAVID points to the center of his chest.

DAVID

…like someone is slowly tightening a metal belt around my chest…and I want it to go away. So please, *stop talking to me,* because it's you, you're tightening the belt Emily; everything that comes out of your mouth…

EMILY

Don't tell me these things.

DAVID

You wanted to know.

EMILY

David, do you love me?

DAVID sits up and looks at EMILY:

DAVID

I told you that I did.

EMILY

But do you really?

DAVID

Yes.

EMILY

Ok, then I want to ask you something—

DAVID

Ok.

EMILY

Do you tell Maisie you love her?

DAVID

I don't want to talk about Maisie anymore.

EMILY

Yes or no, David!

DAVID

Yes.

EMILY

Why?

DAVID

What do you mean, 'why?'

EMILY

I mean: why do you tell her you love her, if love me?

DAVID

I don't know?! It's just something I do! It's something
people do when they're in relationships! I don't know!
don't look so upset! I just don't know!

EMILY

But do you actually *feel love for her*, David? That's what I
want to know, when you say it.

DAVID

No! I don't! Ok.

EMILY

That's what I thought.

DAVID

Let's go to your room—I can't deal with this right now.

EMILY

David...do you really think I'm actually going to sleep with you right now? honestly—

DAVID

Why wouldn't we? It's how we usually deal with our problems!

EMILY

No, it's how we make them.

DAVID

Emily: relationships are complicated...there's miscommunication, and yes, people lie...but I'm not trying to hurt anyone, you're not trying to hurt anyone— so what's the big deal? We give each other pleasure, why can't we enjoy it? Why do we have to torture ourselves?—I just don't get it...I don't see what it accomplishes.

EMILY

First of all: who said I'm not trying to hurt anyone? Second of all: who said you give me pleasure?

DAVID

You can't bring yourself to admit that you're attracted to

me. That you were from the beginning and that you still are.

EMILY

No, I can't.

DAVID

The only difference between you and me, Emily, is that I know what I am and what I like and how to enjoy it. But you don't. Pleasure doesn't work for you because it's too common, too much like the pleasure that people less intelligent, less beautiful than you can have...

EMILY

I already told you that you won, David—ok?

DAVID

You have this ability to paralyze...it's...the idea that we don't share anything meaningful is propaganda, it's pure propaganda—it keeps the status quo alive... I mean, like, think about the emails you send me in the middle of night; the ones that are like five or six pages long—you tell me things Emily; things that are important to you—you tell me more than you tell anybody else I think—

EMILY

It's like writing anonoymous person...to a stranger...it's convenient—don't confuse *that*...for—

DAVID

You're just afraid of what will happen if you stop trying to humiliate me—

EMILY

Calm down.

DAVID

What about the night your brother died: who did you call?
It wasn't your parents, it wasn't a friend, it wasn't Maisie—
it was me. Emily. It was me.

EMILY

How dare you bring up Chris...

DAVID

You *need* to recognize me—

EMILY

Is that a threat?

DAVID

I don't know what it is.

EMILY

You don't have the right to talk about him...I don't care
how unfair I am; it's on not the same level...it's not, it's
not, it's not; I can't take it...

DAVID

I'm sorry if I hurt you.

EMILY

You didn't hurt *me*...that's not the problem.

DAVID

Then what is this conversation about? I want you to tell
me—if it's not about you being hurt.

EMILY

This isn't a conversation, David. This isn't an argument.
This isn't a blood-letting. This isn't the prelude to making
love. This is me divorcing myself from the fantasy of sex
without surrender or submission or sadness. This is me
just saying 'no' so that I can save my own skin... I admit:
I'm the hypocrite. I'm the asshole...are you happy?—
because this is where the movie ends. Roll credits. Finish
your popcorn, take a piss, go home. Cya.

DAVID

What are you trying to say?

EMILY

I'm not trying to say anything...I'm trying to confess my
sins to you...

DAVID

What else is there to confess!?

EMILY

I told you already: bad dreams...

DAVID

Can you say what you mean for once, Emily? I feel like gonna
go crazy...

EMILY

I've been saying what I mean this whole time; love
devalues itself over and over and over; you start with the
old-fashioned common sense feeling of wanting to fuck
someone, or to love them or whatever—and you end up

doing this purely strategic tap-dance…this inscribing of fictions that's semi-judicial in that it layers rule on top of rule without ever actually legislating away that hurt; that self-inflicted hurt that—

DAVID

Emily!

EMILY

Just let me talk—

DAVID

You're not saying words at this point—

EMILY

I'm waiting to be interpreted—

DAVID

It's just wild; you sound wild; there's nothing I can interpret; shit Emily—there's just this unleashing—

EMILY

I've brought you this far just to show you the image of myself…but you keep looking away and I don't know what to do…

DAVID

Just be vulnerable. Just admit that whatever we have between us means something to you.

EMILY

All it means to me is shame.

DAVID

Right, of course...because the only thing that you accept as real between people is shame...and because I don't feel enough shame for your taste, you turn on me, relentlessly... just relentlessly...because you want me to feel as shitty as you do about this...about *sex*...but I don't, I just don't. I'm pathetically, shamelessly happy. And so whatever. Ok? *Whatever*. I'm here, you're here; I want to hook up, you don't. *Whatever*. If you don't want anything...then at least just let me be whatever I am. I don't need to be involved in this game of self-hatred that you like to play. I mean, fuck it, Emily—if my lack of guilt upsets you, then tell Maisie and get it over with—just get it over with; because it's not worth it to me anymore.

Cue: the sound of the door to the building door opening.

EMILY

It's an image for longing, that's what I've tried to show you.

Cue: the sound of steps on the stairs and the jangling of keys.

Exit EMILY running.

Enter MAISIE.

MAISIE looks at DAVID, stricken.

MAISIE

David—you look like someone died.

DAVID
  You didn't answer your phone.

MAISIE
  No.

DAVID
  Why not?

MAISIE
  It was on silent all day…and I forgot about it I guess.

DAVID
  You always respond right away, Maisie.

MAISIE
  Look, David, I'm sorry, but I can't have this conversation
  right now, I'm sorry; I just needed a break from my phone;
  so I took one; that's it.

DAVID
  Look, it's ok. Don't worry about it. I forgive you.

MAISIE
  Did Emily let you in?

DAVID
  Uh…yeah…a while ago.

MAISIE
  Is she still here?

DAVID
  I think she's in her room.

MAISIE

Did you talk to her at all?

DAVID

Not really. The two of us don't have much to say to each other.

MAISIE sits down on the futon and takes DAVID'S hands in her own.

MAISIE

I missed you.

DAVID

Did you?

MAISIE

Yes, of course I missed you.

DAVID

Ok.

MAISIE

You seem upset.

DAVID

I'm just freaking out about work, I guess. I dunno. I just feel stressed out. Anxious. It'll pass.

MAISIE

How long have you been waiting for me?

DAVID

I couldn't tell you.

MAISIE

I feel bad.

DAVID

Why do you feel bad?

MAISIE

Because you've just been sitting here waiting for me: it's sweet.

DAVID looks down.

MAISIE

You're upset about something—

DAVID

No, it's nothing.

MAISIE

Has Emily said something to you?

DAVID

What would she have said Maisie?

MAISIE

I don't know; I don't know why I said that.

DAVID

Fuck.

MAISIE

What's wrong?

DAVID

Just: *fuck.*

MAISIE

Something's wrong.

DAVID

I guess something's wrong—yea.

MAISIE

Are we talking about the same thing?

DAVID

I don't know Maze, are we?

MAISIE

I don't know, David. You're being so vague.

DAVID looks listlessly at his phone.

MAISIE

Look at me.

DAVID

I don't want to look at you right now.

MAISIE

What have I done David? Just tell me! Please—

DAVID

It's nothing you've done.

MAISIE

Yes it is.

DAVID

I promise you, it's not—I'll explain later.

MAISIE

I feel terrible.

MAISIE gets up and goes to the record player.

She puts on a Chopin nocturne (Op.9 #1 in B-flat Minor)

MAISIE

Don't you think it's pretty?

DAVID shrugs.

MAISIE

Are you sure you're ok?

DAVID

No.

MAISIE

David: what did I do?—can you please tell me?

DAVID

Why do you think it's something you've done?

MAISIE

I don't know.

DAVID

Hey…look—I think I'm gonna go.

MAISIE

Aren't you going to tell me what's going on?

DAVID

Aren't you going to tell me?

MAISIE

No.

DAVID stands up.

DAVID

That's what I thought.

MAISIE

Respect just covers up the void where love used to be, don't you think?—like drawn blinds.

DAVID

Cya, Maze.

MAISIE steps back, biting her lip, looking at him instead of kissing him goodbye.

Exit DAVID.

MAISIE gets up, running her hands through her hair, looking dazed.

Lights down.

MUSIC continues through beginning of ACT III and fades.

ACT III

Stage is dark.

MAX and MAISIE enter stage in the dark, finding their way without light.

We hear the sound of MAISIE putting her purse on the kitchen table.

Lamp next to futon gets switched on and MAISIE sits down while MAX remains in the doorway.

MAX

When it started to rain tonight, and we were sitting in the cafe, and you opened your hand to me like a flower—it was like you were telling me a secret, but I forgot to ask you what it was.

MAISIE

Can you please come over here and sit with me?

MAX closes the door, slowly and carefully, and sits down next to her.

MAISIE

I don't remember the last time I've wanted to be kissed like this—

MAX kisses her.

MAISIE

It's dizziness...

MAX kisses her again.

MAISIE (cont'd)
  It's mortifying.

MAX
  Why did you ask me tonight if I was seeing anybody else?

MAISIE
  Because you never said if you were or not.

MAX
  Well I'm not.

MAISIE
  But you could've been.

MAX
  That's true.

MAISIE
  And you could meet someone else tomorrow.

MAX
  I won't.

MAISIE
  But you could.

MAX
  And so could you.

MAISIE
  But I won't.

MAX

I feel apprehensive.

MAISIE

I don't want you to feel apprehensive.

MAX

But I do.

MAISIE

Why? I want you to feel like you're in the right place.

MAX

I do, that's why I'm apprehensive.

MAISIE

Why would that make you apprehensive?

MAX

Because it means I'm considering letting my guard down.

MAISIE

Oh you should! Let's not be guarded. Let's stay up and talk. I'll make some coffee!

MAISIE leaps up.

MAX

I want to know why you haven't left David yet—

MAISIE

I told you!

MAX

Not really. You just said that you hadn't seen him since yesterday.

MAISIE

I need some time.

MAX

I'm sorry, I'm being pushy.

MAISIE

Yes, you are—

MAX

I just feel like you're never going to tell him.

MAISIE

I have no way of proving that to you.

MAX

You could call him right now.

MAISIE

I can't break up with him over the phone!

MAX

Why not?

MAISIE

Because that would be divorcing myself from the reality of him and that's something...that's something I've already done isn't it?

MAX
  You tell me—

MAISIE
  It is.

MAX
  So call him then—

MAISIE
  No, I still can't.

MAX
  Why not?

MAISIE
  Because you're telling me to, and I always do the opposite
  of what people tell me to do.

MAX
  So do I, incidentally.

MAISIE
  So maybe we shouldn't tell each other to do things—

MAX
  It doesn't matter either way.

MAISIE
  Why are you being so fatalistic?

MAX
  Why are you?

MAISIE

You think I'm fatalistic?

MAX

At least about romantic love.

MAISIE

Romantic love is not my idea of a good time.

MAX

I'm not talking about having a good time.

MAISIE

What are you talking about then?

MAX

Tracing the dense spirals of infinity that grow inside of each person, like a second skeleton.

MAISIE

I don't love words the way you do...

MAX

You don't have to—

MAISIE

But what if I feel like I should?

MAX

Just ignore that feeling—

MAISIE

You feel like a controlling person. Are you a controlling person Max?

MAX

You're trying to find something wrong with me.

MAISIE

Of course I am—

MAX

It's like you want me to be weaker than I really am—

MAISIE

Yes. Because it's so unfair of you not to show any weakness.
It's ridiculous! People shouldn't be so self-sufficient...

MAX

Believe me, I'm not.

MAISIE

Of course you are.

MAX

You only say that because you don't know me very well.

MAISIE

I need to be able to feel safe around you.

MAX

Then go ahead: feel safe.

MAISIE

No, I need you to show me that you can be hurt by me the
same way I can be hurt by you. I'm afraid of getting hurt
by you.

MAX

Who cares? you get hurt—so what?

MAISIE

Why should I want that?

MAX

Because it'd be something new! I don't know! It's just life—loving and hurting...and I don't want to shy away from it.

MAISIE

I'm not used to being with someone who's so romantic.

MAX

I'm not being romantic, I'm realistic.

MAISIE

No, you're being completely unrealistic, and that's what scares me.

MAX

Yesterday you liked that I was emotional, today it scares you that I'm romantic.

MAISIE

Well I was braver yesterday.

MAX

Why?

MAISIE

Because that was all the bravery I had; I used it up, and now it's time to be scared again.

MAX

I like you.

MAISIE

I'm not sleeping with you right now—I hope you know
that.

MAX

Ok.

MAISIE

Are you disappointed with me?

MAX

No.

MAISIE

What are you thinking about?

MAX

When I was a kid, my grandfather used to take me hunting.
He liked to take me out early in the morning, especially
when it was very cold outside. Whenever he shot a buck,
he would hang it upside down from an oak tree outside his
house...a dead buck has silver eyes...eyes that are always
on the verge of going totally black...I would spend entire
afternoons watching those eyes, convinced that they would
come alive again...You don't know why I'm telling you this
story, but that's ok; you think of me as one kind of person;
but the truth is, I'm several kinds of people all at once, just
like you are—just like everyone is—

Enter EMILY from her bedroom offstage.

MAX and MAISIE look up, startled.

EMILY

Don't look so concerned, I'm just getting some water and going back to bed.

EMILY gets a glass and fills it from a pitcher on the counter.

EMILY leans back against the counter and looks at MAX and MAISIE.

EMILY (cont'd)

Hey, don't look so happy to see me guys.

MAISIE

We were in the middle of a conversation…

EMILY

Well, I was in the middle of getting water.

MAISIE stands up.

MAISIE

I feel like being alone right now. Emily stay and keep Max company.

Exit MAISIE with considerable awkwardness.

MAX, looking uneasy, remains on the futon.

EMILY

Aren't you going to follow her?

MAX

I'll get around to it.

Cue: the sound of MAISIE practicing the viola.

EMILY goes and sits next to MAX on the futon.

EMILY

Are you two fighting?

MAX

No.

EMILY

Then what are you doing?

MAX

Talking.

EMILY

So you're fighting—

MAX

Talking. We're just talking.

EMILY

Talking means fighting. Even if you're not fighting, you're fighting.

MAX

Well, if you put it that way.

EMILY

She doesn't seem very happy.

MAX

She has some things to figure out.

EMILY

Like what?

MAX

I don't need to explain—

EMILY

Sure you do—

MAX

No, I don't think I do.

EMILY

You are really pretentious, you know that?

MAX

I'll take your word for it.

EMILY

And I bet you're working on a novel about a sensitive young man who just wants to be taken seriously as an artist and just wants his father's approval—

MAX

I'm not going to flirt with you Emily—

EMILY

Uhuh.

She begins to play with his hair.

EMILY

You've got very pretty hair. You must have tousled it extensively before coming over tonight.

MAX breaks away from her touch.

EMILY

Don't be so surly.

MAX

I just don't like how predictable this is.

EMILY

What's so predictable about this?

MAX

Your attempting to prove that you're more alluring than her.

EMILY

That's mean.

MAX

You bet it is.

EMILY

Then why did you say it?

MAX

Because you want me to be mean to you.

EMILY

Hey, why don't you just let me play with your hair and shut up?

MAX

She's right there, Emily—

EMILY

    (hushed)

So what?

MAX

So what? You're not worth losing her—

EMILY

Don't be mean.

MAX

Don't touch me.

EMILY

But the room is already littered with kisses, who would notice a few more?

MAX

I would.

EMILY

That's too bad.

MAX

I thought you were going back to bed.

EMILY

Well, you've got me all worked up. And besides, your lady-love is intent on expressing herself through song.

MAX

I'm telling you Emily, this doesn't impress me—

EMILY

What doesn't impress you?

MAX

Manneristic cruelty.

EMILY

You think *this* is being cruel?

MAX

Yes.

EMILY

But you like it—

MAX

Like I said, it doesn't matter whether I do or I don't.

EMILY

Then why are you talking to me in here and not her in there?

MAX

Well, she told me to stay in here and talk to you.

EMILY

Oh don't pretend like that didn't mean something else.

MAX

What did it mean then?

    The music stops.

They look at each other.

The music starts again.

MAX sits up.

EMILY

It meant that she wanted you to follow her.

MAX

No, it meant that she'd given up on me.

EMILY

Why are you out here Max? Just tell me.

MAX

Each person is a new mood...I can't explain it. You walk in the room, the mood changes, and I want to understand it before I leave...I have to understand it before I leave—

EMILY

Maybe you're waiting for something exciting to happen.

MAX

Maybe I am.

EMILY

And maybe that's what I'm waiting for too.

MAX

Maybe it is.

EMILY

And what about her?

MAX

She's waiting too.

EMILY

No, she's not waiting for anyone Max; the exciting thing's already happened for her—and it's you.

MAX

She's already bored of me, I think.

EMILY

She really likes you, you know.

MAX

No, I don't think so—I don't think she likes anyone.

EMILY

Because no one is good enough for her—

MAX

No, and they couldn't be. And she knows it. She doesn't say it, she won't ever say it, but she knows it...

The music stops again.

The lights go off in the bedroom offstage.

EMILY

Looks like she's going to sleep without you—

MAX

I'm not surprised.

EMILY

I don't know why I'm so attracted to you.

MAX
  Please don't—

EMILY
  She's a heavy sleeper—

MAX
  How would you know?

EMILY
  I do a lot of sneaking around.

MAX
  I find this disturbing.

EMILY
  Liar.

MAX
  I do.

EMILY
  Admit that you're lying.

MAX
  But I'm not lying.

EMILY
  Say that you are for my sake—

MAX
  Emily—

EMILY
  What?

MAX

This isn't real.

EMILY

What isn't?

MAX

The intimacy in this room.

EMILY

It would be nice if it was though.

MAX

I just don't know why you're here. I don't know why you're touching me.

EMILY

Just for the static electricity...for the shock of feeling you recoil—

MAX

I'm not recoiling.

EMILY

What are you doing then?

MAX

Sitting here, waiting for Maisie to come back and ask you to leave.

EMILY

And what if she doesn't?

MAX

You're unbelievable…

EMILY

No, I just do what I whatever I want to do.

MAX

And that's what's so unbelievable about you: because I don't think actually you do anything you want to do.

EMILY

Fascinating insight.

MAX doesn't respond.

EMILY (cont'd)

I don't know what to do when you don't talk.

MAX

Just listen.

EMILY

To what?

MAX

The not-talking.

EMILY

I'm afraid of what I'll hear.

MAX starts to whistle.

EMILY

If you weren't here, I could paint.

MAX

Sorry.

EMILY

My eyes and brain are always awake. So painting keeps me from going crazy.

MAX

I said I'm sorry.

EMILY

Painting is the only way I can avoid being trivial.

MAX

Yeah, I get it.

EMILY

The order in which people meet is so arbitrary, but it ends up being incredibly meaningful when it comes to right and wrong.

MAX

Nothing is going to happen—

EMILY

Words just mutilate the feeling, don't they?

MAX

Yup.

They sit in silence for a moment.

EMILY

You know, it doesn't make me feel better about myself to

act like I'm smarter than other people—but I'm guessing that it's the only thing that makes you feel good.

MAX

It doesn't make me feel good Emily—

EMILY

Oh yes it does: I can just feel how much self-satisfaction you gain through feeling like you've thought through things a little more thoroughly than everybody else... but it's such bullshit; like—do you really think you're the only person in the history of the world to speak French or pronounce 'espresso' correctly? Like do you really think any of that makes you any less fragile than anybody else? Any less prone to being a selfish, self-justifying asshole? because guess what Max?—brilliant people die the same way that ordinary people do, which is instantly and forever—ok? So it's nothing to be proud of—

MAX

I don't speak French—

EMILY

And you probably feel incredibly guilty about it—

MAX

Emily—*you don't know me*. You don't know anything about me—*anything*. And you don't want to know, because you're too busy securing yourself against me; too busy making sure that you don't feel vulnerable to something I might have to say. You're eroticizing the moment because that's what you know how to do, not because it's what you like. All you're doing is adjusting the thermostat in the room you've forced yourself into; making sure that the temperature is just right for you and your random bitterness towards people, towards men—

EMILY

If you won't let me make assumptions about you, then don't make assumptions about me.

MAX

Fine...

EMILY

One night, last winter, a few weeks after Maisie moved in with me, we were sitting on the couch, listening to her records, reading, not saying anything to each other, just enjoying the quiet, and it started to snow—and I swear to God this is true—without saying a word, she put down her book and ran outside and started dancing and doing cartwheels and making snow-angels in the street. I was watching her from all the way up here, and I lost it; I mean, I really started to cry...I don't believe in saints or birds or holiness...so when I see people who really believe in the things I've given up on, I...I don't know...I don't know what to do. Why are you looking at me like that?

MAX

Because I'm an idiot.

EMILY

Why are you an idiot?

MAX

Because I feel like you understand me and that I understand you.

EMILY

Yeah.

MAX

But we don't...we don't...we're letting a fantasy spin itself out, and I know it, and I can't really stop it, or don't want to yet.

EMILY

Stop pretending like you're searching for the right answer—

MAX

What?

EMILY

You already know what you want.

MAX

And what do I want?

EMILY

You want Maisie and you want me.

MAX

Can you please tell me why you're out here again?

EMILY

Because thus far, no one's stopped me, or kicked me out.

MAX

That's fair.

*EMILY kisses MAX on the neck and then pulls away
from him.*

EMILY

You're the one doing all the seducing here, just so you know,
not me. And you're getting away with it by pretending you
have some kind of integrity...but you don't...you're just
maintaining your precious self-image at my expense...it's
fucking ruthless...I'll admit that you intuit people pretty
well, but you aren't actually interested in them in any kind
of deep way, except as intellectual projects. I don't need
to know anything about you to see that's true—it was the
first thing I noticed the other morning: how you were just
sitting there thinking while Maisie was actually moved by
love for you—and do you want to know why she seems
so ambivalent about you? It's because you were secretly
ambivalent about her first, and just managed to convince
her that she was the source of the ambivalence, and not
you—

Cue: sound of door opening.

MAX and EMILY react uncomfortably.

Enter MAISIE at edge of stage doorway.

MAISIE

Emily, do you mind giving us some privacy?

EMILY stands up.

EMILY

What for?

MAISIE

Because I'm asking you.

EMILY

But I don't feel tired anymore.

MAISIE

Emily—

EMILY

I understand, you want to be alone with young Kierkegaard here, but—

MAISIE

Emily—

EMILY

Ok, ok. I get it. I'm a negative presence. And look! I'm [*yawning*] suddenly sleepy again. So goodnight. Sweet dreams everyone.

Exit EMILY.

MAISIE sits next to MAX on the floor.

MAISIE

Max, can you tell me something?

MAX

Yes.

MAISIE

Do you really think that I'll stay with David?

MAX

All I can say, is: why bother to break in a new pair of jeans when you've got a perfectly good pair already, you know?

MAISIE

You and David aren't two of the same thing.

MAX

I'm not so sure about that.

MAISIE

No, you're not, Max! I promise.

MAX

Then break up with him Maisie. Jump, I'll follow.

MAISIE

But I'm afraid to. And...you don't really look like someone who is ready to jump after me—

MAX

What do I look like then?

MAISIE

Like someone who's already in the process of falling—

MAX

Yeah, that seems about right.

MAISIE
Why won't you make eye-contact with me?

MAX
I'm not here, I don't think.

MAISIE
Then where are you?

MAX
Everywhere but here.

MAISIE
Where did you go?

MAX
Away.

MAISIE
Oh.

MAX
I'll try to make my way back. If I can—

MAISIE
I've ignored David all day, just so you know.

MAX
Alright.

MAISIE
Doesn't that mean anything to you?

MAX

Today it means something. But what about tomorrow, and the next day? And the next—

MAISIE

He'll give up. He'll get the message.

MAX

No, he'll show up here.

MAISIE

Do you think Emily told him about us?

MAX

Yes.

MAISIE

You're positive?

MAX

Yes.

MAISIE

What did she tell you?

MAX

Nothing. It's just a hunch—

MAISIE

I'd hoped she'd say something…

MAX

That's why you left us out here?—

MAISIE

That was part of it.

MAX

And what was the other part? Did you want to see if something would happen between us?

MAISIE

I just wanted to see if it was possible!

MAX

Were you listening?

MAISIE

I don't know!

MAX

You don't know if you were listening or not?!

MAISIE

What does it matter?

MAX

What does it matter? *Maisie*...never mind.

MAISIE

Tell me!

MAX

I need to know if you were listening or not—

MAISIE

I didn't need to listen.

MAX

What do you mean?

MAISIE

Because I was trying to teach myself how to have faith.

MAX

But we communicate like we're negotiating a peace treaty, Maisie—that's the opposite of faith. Faith means sitting in silence. It means not asking questions.

MAISIE

I was sitting in silence. I'm not asking questions.

MAX

No, you're not asking questions, because you've already made up your mind about me.

MAISIE

Max—

MAX

What?

MAISIE

I played the viola, I put it down, I turned off the lights, I put on headphones, I counted to 400 and then I came back out here, and what I saw were two people who were incredibly relieved that they weren't alone anymore.

MAX

I'm sorry—

MAISIE

Don't worry, I know that nothing happened…but I also know that I kind of wish that something had—and that you do too.

MAX

I really don't.

MAISIE

You should though—

MAX

Why do you keep saying things like that? Why are you acting like I'd be happier with Emily?

MAISIE

I'm not fun to be around; I'm insecure, defensive, distrustful—

MAX

That's not true—

MAISIE

What if it is?

MAX

It's not—

MAISIE

But I'll never stop believing that it is.

MAX

I really don't know how to convince you otherwise. I don't

know how to make you see that I'm risking being hurt by you because I think you're worth it—

MAISIE

Will I ever wake up and feel okay with the mediocrity and complacency I've programmed myself to take comfort in?

MAX

I don't know.

MAISIE

You have an answer for everything except for the one question I genuinely want an answer to.

MAX

What you want is to live with devotion and grace...but that only comes through constant experiment; random leaps and dizzying falls.

MAISIE

That sounds dangerous.

MAX

It is.

MAISIE

I want to cultivate the uncertainty which haunts me...the lingering thoughts, the loose associations, the meandering sentences. I want feeling, I want *lyricism*...I want to start taking risks...but, when I think about it...I just can't bring myself to hurt David...I just can't—

MAX

You want to make sure that you can still go back to him if you change your mind about me.

MAISIE

I care about you so much Max—

MAX

Then you have to choose me.

MAISIE

I'm trying my best.

MAX

What you're doing is the opposite of choosing: you're leaving all of your options open.

MAISIE

What are you feeling?

MAX

Falsified.

MAISIE

You look so sad—

MAX

I just wasn't prepared—I've never felt so unprepared for anything in my whole life.

MAISIE

Unprepared for what?

MAX

For you.

MAISIE

And what am I?

MAX

Incomparably alive. Astoundingly alive.

MAISIE

What else?

MAX

Selfish.

MAISIE

I can't help it.

MAX

Being selfish?

MAISIE

Yes, being selfish.

MAX

I'm not trying to make you feel bad—

MAISIE

I bear the wounds of displacement; of having fled myself...

MAX

All you have to do is walk back into your own light.

MAISIE

You'll find someone you like better than me—and you'll forget we even had this conversation—

MAX

What exactly is 'this conversation'?

MAISIE

The one where I launch myself into the emptiness of not wanting anything from anyone.

MAX

Maisie, I'd climb up to your roof, I'd wipe away the light pollution and say: 'look at all of these impossible stars'... but I'm not sure if either of us remembers how to believe in stars enough to see them anymore.

MAISIE

Because it's simpler that way.

MAX

No, it's so much more complicated.

MAISIE

When we met up tonight, all I wanted to do was run away.

MAX

Then why didn't you?

MAISIE

Because at the time, I was more afraid of running than of staying.

MAX

What's the point of all the beauty in our lives if the contact doesn't yield any permanent change; if we don't gain any courage through it?

MAISIE

I just don't know anyone else who talks like you...

MAX

How do I talk?

MAISIE

You talk around problems and straight into them at the same time...it's like your brain is emotional. You have an emotional brain, or a brainy heart—or something. It just makes me so nervous.

MAX

Everything makes you nervous...

MAISIE

Can you please accept that I'm weaker than you?

MAX

No.

MAISIE

Then why are you still judging me—why are you still sitting there, all emotional, all broken up—still judging me...it's *horrible*.

MAX

I'm not doing anything.

MAISIE

It's like I have no privacy when you look at me. I feel the same way when I'm with Emily.

MAX

How could I possibly prove to you that that's not true?

MAISIE

You couldn't, because it's true.

MAX

Just like with Emily?

MAISIE

Yes.

MAX

Ok…I gotta go: I'm sorry.

MAX motions to leave.

MAISIE

Max!

MAX stops.

MAX

What?

MAISIE

Just put up with me, ok? I don't have experience with choosing. But I'll try to learn.

MAX

But what am I putting up with exactly?

MAISIE

My pushing you away.

MAX

Ok...ok.

MAISIE gets up and joins MAX and leads MAX to the table again, where they both sit down, their hands intertwined.

MAISIE

Do you think Emily told David about us? I need to know! It's killing me—

MAX

Fuck—Maisie, I told you: yes.

MAISIE

I refuse to believe it.

MAX

But it's a good thing—isn't it?

MAISIE

It's good for you—

MAX

It has nothing to do with me. The point is: if Emily told David about us, you don't have to lie, or anything. You just have to let him go.

MAISIE

Don't act like it's easy to end a relationship...

MAX

Trust me, I'm not saying I'm above any of this, I'm just telling you what the situation is—

MAISIE

I just want to know how can you be so sure Emily told him.

MAX

How can you not be?

MAISIE

Because I don't want to be.

MAX

Exactly.

MAISIE

I don't know why you say the things you do Max. Like, how could you possibly have such a strong intuition about Emily? She must have told you something. I feel like everyone knows something that I don't...you all say you're intuitive, but it's more than that. Emily *said something to you Max*.

MAX

She didn't. I promise you I'm telling the truth.

MAISIE

But still, there's something you're not saying! And I want to know what it is!

MAX

Tell me why you quit music school—

MAISIE

I'm not talking about that now.

MAX

Why not?

MAISIE

Because I'm just not.

MAX

I want to know—

MAISIE

You're doing it again Max!

MAX

Doing what?

MAISIE

Looking through the drawers—you need to stop.

MAX

Do you wanna know, Maisie, why you feel like there are all these things that nobody is telling you? It's because you're not paying any attention to what's around you and other people are! Do you wanna know why I'm so sure Emily told David about us? because it's obvious that she's jealous of you and that telling David is her only way of getting even. It's just obvious Maisie! It's the first thing you'd see if you opened your eyes.

MAISIE

You hurt me so much.

MAX momentarily puts his head in his hands and then looks back at MAISIE.

MAX

I know...I know. I should have let this be a one-night thing. Really. I was selfish and insistent, when you knew better...

MAISIE

Maybe I'm really as innocent as you and Emily say.

MAX

Stand up.

MAISIE

What?

MAX

Stand up.

They both stand up from the table.

MAX takes her hands in his.

MAX

Maisie: we're being ridiculous.

MAISIE

I know.

MAX

All we have to do is just say we love each other and that we
trust each other; can you just say that to me?

MAISIE

Yes.

MAX

Then say it.

MAISIE

I love you. I trust you…Now you say it.

MAX

I love you. I trust you.

MAISIE

Are you happy now?

MAX

I'm getting there.

MAISIE

Can you go now?

MAX looks at her in disbelief.

MAX

Say that again?

MAISIE

I said: can you go now?—please.

MAX

Maisie—

MAISIE

Please.

MAX

Are you really serious?—you want me to leave.

MAISIE

Please.

MAX chuckles slightly and shakes his head in disbelief.

MAISIE (cont'd)

You shouldn't have let me leave you alone with Emily.

MAX

Maisie—

MAISIE

And you shouldn't have shown me so much emotion; I'm not used to it; I can't completely handle it—

MAX

I really, really don't want to leave.

MAISIE

Still, you have to.

MAX

I feel a pit in my stomach.

MAISIE

Me too Max; I'm sorry.

MAX

I want to keep talking.

MAISIE

I feel really tired.

MAX

You don't seem tired.

MAISIE

Max, I'm sorry.

MAX

Maisie…

MAISIE

You have to listen to me. This is too intense…I told you I love you—that has to be enough for now…I'll text you later, ok?…ok?…Why are you laughing like that?

MAX

Just because.

MAISIE kisses Max briefly and goes back to the futon.

MAISIE

Please don't hate me.

MAX goes to the door.

MAISIE

Can you turn the lights out on your way out?

MAX turns out the light.

The door shuts.

MAISIE goes to the center of the room/stage.

MAISIE turns on a lamp.

MAISIE goes to the record player and puts on the Chopin record back on at low volume (Nocturne in C minor, Op #48).

MAISIE goes back to the table, picks up her purse, takes out her phone, puts the phone to her ear, and leans against the table facing the audience. She begins to talk to an answering machine.

MAISIE

Hi, it's me...your phone is off right now...so I guess I'm just gonna talk and see what happens...because I know that I've been showing serious signs of being hurt, or wanting to hurt, or whatever; both I guess...maybe wanting to hurt more than anything...and I'm saying this because I want to explain myself, or want you to listen to me explain myself all the way through to the end of this feeling I have right now...because listening is a gesture you know, like waving goodbye or kissing someone on the cheek...and because I want you to understand for your own sake, so that I can stop understanding for you...and, honestly, I don't believe any of this as I'm saying it, but by the end of this message I'm going to believe it and you are too, because that's all people can do for each other you know, believe for the sake of it; believe for the sake of keeping warm during a long summer of sleep, death, desire...but really, I just wanted to say that yesterday I woke up to play the viola while the sun was coming up, and that it was the first time I'd really played music in a year, and that I realized, even though I didn't tell anyone, that music, which I've always thought of as 'the only thing that matters' doesn't measure up to the wonder of a voice, the human voice itself, as it speaks and is filled with and is nothing but LOVE, in regards to another person, like you, I mean…because I dearly dearly want to have faith in someone because that's all that matters, right? Having faith, and everything—because the sun as it was coming up told me this and the music I heard not only out loud but inside too, where music begins and ends, repeated it; said 'have faith'…and so I guess I'm sorry I ignored you today, I really am, I've never done that before and it was mean and disrespectful because you just wanted to know where I was and if I was ok…so if you hear this, can you forgive me and please come over? Because I don't want to sleep alone tonight and I'm not feeling tired at all. I could stay awake all night. I think I will anyway. I want to see you. I want you to come over. I want to be with you David.

Lights down.

www.ingramcontent.com/pod-product-compliance
Lightning Source LLC
LaVergne TN
LVHW041221080426
835508LV00011B/1034